Guess What

is in

Grandma's Garden?

written by **Nancy O'Neill**
illustrated by **Kids Around the World**

Cover design: Nancy O'Neill
Color illustrations: Kids Around the World

First printing: May 2014
Printed in the United States.

ISBN 13: 978-1496115638
ISBN 10: 1496115635

Proceeds from this book help support Rady Children's Hospital in San Diego, California.

The Illustrators

Talented young artists are all around us if we just give them an opportunity to be creative. I am proud to feature the following kids' artwork in my book. These artists used soft pastels, watercolors, colored pencils, tempera paint, and brush markers.

Listed in the order their artwork appears in the book:

Rachelle Marie Escaner Lariba	14	Kapolei, HI
Sonja Matienzo	14	California
Cindy Tsou	13	Kapolei, HI
Tamara Acevedo	12	New London, CT
Aidyn K. H.	12	Kapolei, HI
Abby McGuire	14	Ladera Ranch, CA
Eliza A. Crowley	14	Yarmouth, ME
Sophia K. Cleek	13	Kapolei, HI
Leya Ann Leliaert	13	Kapolei, HI
Macey M. Fleming	14	Cincinnati, OH
Aditi Girish Laddha	17	Indore, Madhya Pradesh, India
Isaac Badua	13	Kapolei, HI
Lili Wysocka	10	Wejherowo, Poland

You can read more about these young artists on my website at guesswhatbooks.com as well as see the list of other talented kids who submitted artwork for the contest.

Thank you from the bottom of my heart. I appreciate each one of you.

Nancy O'Neill

The Dedication

This book is dedicated to my mom. At 80 years old, with help from my dad, Mom still plants two large gardens on their ranch, even though they end up with more fruits and vegetables than they could ever possibly eat. She preserves many of the vegetables through a canning process so they have garden vegetables throughout the harsh North Dakota winters. Some of the produce is sold to people who don't plant gardens or is traded with other farmers who grow or raise things that she doesn't. Mom also donates produce to their local Senior Citizen Center.

She likes to stay busy and says that the garden gives her something to do. Her love for gardening gave me the idea for this book. Thanks, Mom.

The Acknowledgments

Just like Mom's garden, my book series continues to grow organically. With this fourth book in print, I am so grateful that I have the support and encouragement from my family and friends. A special thanks to Don and Jason for always being there for me. You are why I am able to do what I love to do.

The seeds were planted in the spring,
Then watered so they'd grow.
Now it's time to see what's here,
And how many things you know.

Shades of red and speckled with seeds,
This fruit is very sweet.
It grows on plants that lay down low.
Let's pick some, then we'll eat.

Strawberries
Rachelle Marie Escaner Lariba – Age 14

They're orange and grow beneath the ground,
With leafy green stems on top.
Rabbits like to munch on these.
Grandma wishes they'd stop.

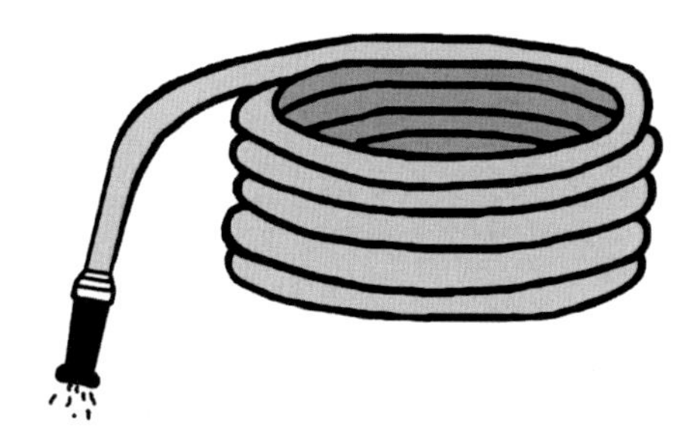

Carrots

Sonja Matienzo – Age 14

On a sandwich or salad plate,
It's almost always green.
Give me bacon and tomato,
With this green leaf in between.

Lettuce

Cindy Tsou – Age 13

Grandma's garden has so much more.
Let's see what summer brings.
This insect flies from plant to plant,
And flaps its colorful wings.

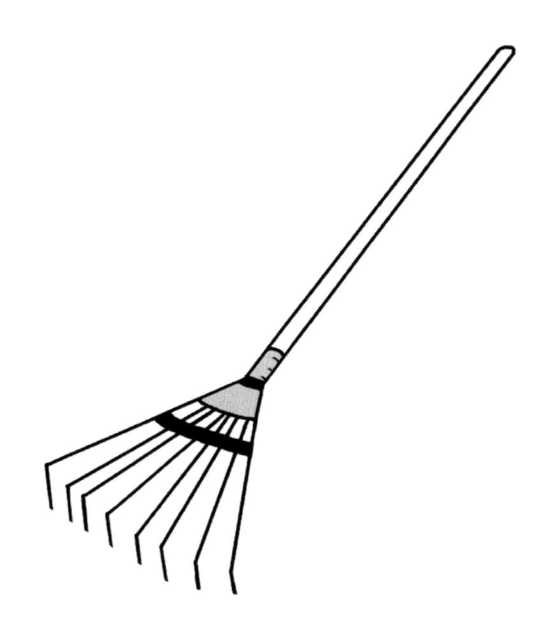

Butterfly

Tamara Acevedo – Age 12

Top a burger with one of these,
So red and thinly sliced.
They're also good in other foods,
When stewed or even diced.

Tomatoes

Aidyn K. H. – Age 12

They're often carved at Halloween,
With noses, mouths, and eyes.
Orange outside and orange within,
They make delicious pies.

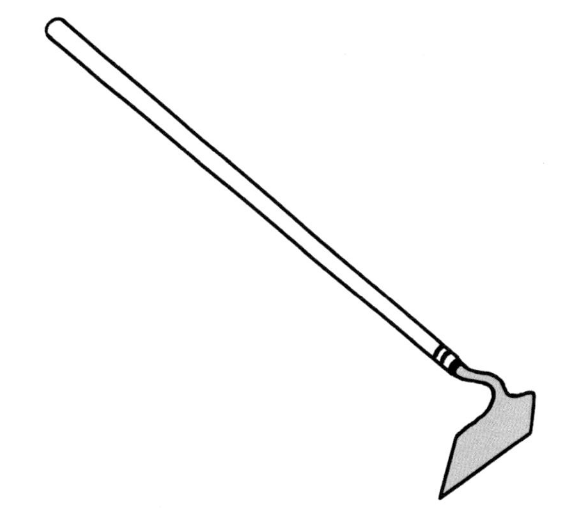

Pumpkins

Abby McGuire – Age 14

When chopping these to spice up foods,
Grandma starts to cry.
A veggie that can make her tear.
Do you wonder why?

Onions

Eliza A. Crowley – Age 14

A small red bug with round black spots,
And wings so it can fly.
It eats the insects from the plants,
Then takes off to the sky.

Ladybug

Sophia K. Cleek – Age 13

No matter if it's raw or cooked,
It looks like small green trees.
Good with butter or eaten plain,
Or topped with melted cheese.

Broccoli

Leya Ann Leliaert – Age 13

They have eyes but cannot see,
The taste just can't be beat.
Baked or mashed or often fried,
Some are even sweet.

Potatoes

Macey M. Fleming – Age 14

Full of water and juicy red,
With thick green outer skin.
Some have black seeds, some have white,
And some have none within.

Watermelon

Aditi Girish Laddha – Age 17

Frozen, canned, or on the cob,
It can even pop.
No matter how you eat it,
It's good with butter on top.

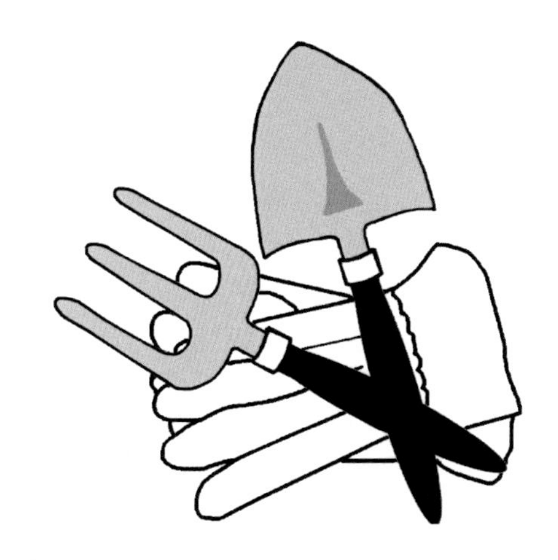

Corn on the cob

Isaac Badua – Age 13

Dressed in clothes and wearing a hat,
It's stuffed with straw or hay.
Propped up straight beside a stick,
It scares the birds away.

Scarecrow
Lili Wysocka – Age 10

That's what Grandma's garden has,
And now we're almost done.
Of all the things we saw today,
What was your favorite one?

The Contest

One of Nancy O'Neill's passions is helping kids explore possibilities and opportunities. This is what sparked the idea of having a contest to feature kids' artwork in her Guess What books. Not only would kids have worldwide recognition for their talent and accomplishments but it could present opportunities that they may never have imagined.

Creativity has no boundaries which is why each contest is open to kids around the world. Once a manuscript is finished for each book in the series, a new Kids Art Contest begins. Thirteen specific illustrations are needed for each book. Young artists are encouraged to submit multiple illustrations as that increases their chances of one of their drawings being selected. Unfortunately, multiple submissions cannot guarantee that one will be chosen.

Opportunities are endless so whether a child's artwork is chosen or not, they are still eligible to submit illustrations for future Guess What books.

For submission guidelines or to receive advance notice when a new art contest begins, please visit guesswhatbooks.com and subscribe to the newsletter.

The Author

Nancy O'Neill grew up on a farm in the middle of North Dakota. Over the years, her family raised beef cattle, dairy cows, chickens, pigs, and sheep as well as grew a variety of field crops. They also had a few ponies and always a dog or two, plus many barn cats. Nancy learned how to milk cows, pick eggs, and drive a tractor to rake hay in the field. She also helped plant gardens every spring, picked weeds all summer, and then helped harvest the vegetables in the fall. To this day, her parents still plant gardens, which is what prompted the theme for this book.

Having a Midwestern background has given Nancy a solid foundation for everything she has accomplished thus far. She has always gravitated toward anything creative but also likes tech-related challenges. She considers herself a techie geek girl even though she grew up long before the technology era.

Her writing career began with poetry, short stories, and articles about many topics while she was working in the corporate world. After the birth of her son, she left the traditional job market to become a stay-at-home mom and discovered a new-found love for writing children's stories.

In addition to her own books, she also offers self-publishing services to other authors. Nancy has worked on memoirs, business books, inspirational books, children's books for all ages, and a cookbook for a non-profit organization. She has also ghostwritten for several authors.

Nancy enjoys being a mom, wife, author, and entrepreneur. She lives in southern California with her husband and teenage son.

Upcoming Books

Watch for the fifth Guess What book,
Guess What is in the Ocean?

And Guess What?

You just never know where the next adventure may take you.

The first three books in the series are available on
Amazon, Barnes & Noble, and other online retailers.
You can also purchase autographed copies at
www.guesswhatbooks.com.

Guess What is on Grandpa's Farm?
Guess What is at the North Pole?
Guess What is at the Zoo? (Winner of The Gittle List for 2013)

Made in the USA
Columbia, SC
26 October 2021